FOR YOUR HOME

HOME OFFICES

FOR YOUR HOME

HOME OFFICES

Lisa Sholnik

FRIEDMAN/FAIRFAX
PUBLISHERS

Dedication

For Howard, who shares my heart and home office

Acknowledgments

Thank you to the staff at Michael Friedman Publishing Group,

particularly my talented and meticulous editor, Hallie Einhorn.

A FRIEDMAN/FAIRFAX BOOK

© 1995 by Michael Friedman Publishing Group, Inc.

Library of Congress Cataloging-in Publication Data available upon request

ISBN 1-56799-267-6

Editor: Hallie Einhorn
Art Director: Jeff Batzli
Designer: Lynne Yeamans
Photography Editor: Emilya Naymark
Production Associate: Camille Lee

Color separations by Fine Arts Repro House Co., Ltd.
Printed in China by Leefung-Asco Printers Ltd.

For bulk purchases and special sales, please contact:
Friedman/Fairfax Publishers
Attention: Sales Department
15 West 26th Street
New York, New York 10010
212/685-6610   FAX 212/685-1307

Table of Contents

INTRODUCTION

Millions of people are going home to work, either full-time or part-time, and that number is growing every day. In the United States, the actual figure now tops forty-five million people and is expected to reach close to sixty million in just a few years, says Link Resources, a New York research firm that compiles an annual work-at-home survey. The "electronic cottagers" that Alvin Toffler envisioned back in 1980 and the "hoffices" (home/offices) that Faith Popcorn anticipated in 1989 are now upon us.

Ironically, the notion of working at home is not new. Merchants and artisans have labored out of their residences all through the ages. Not until the Industrial Revolution did this standard change, since the demand for employees to staff offices and factories drew people from their homes to central workplaces.

But just as technology revolutionized the way we lived and worked in the nineteenth century, it is doing so once again, and the base of our economy is changing from industry to information. Instead of using heavy machinery, we can work on computers, which are far more compact and mobile. And thanks to the microchip, which has made home computing easy and efficient, the hardware that holds all the data we need is significantly smaller than ever before. Further technological advances, including fax machines, modems, voice mail systems, productivity software, and electronic mail, can be used just as easily in the home as in corporate environments. An office can be placed practically anywhere today, so we have come full circle and are returning to the home.

And for good reason. Who can resist a thirty-second commute? Or wearing exactly what one wants to work? Or better yet, who can turn down the prospect of working in his or her own abode, toiling away while comfortably ensconced in a tailor-made milieu? Furniture and

Opposite: AT THE FAR END OF A DRAMATIC GREAT ROOM, COMPLETE WITH A SWEEPING OVERHANG FROM THE SECOND STORY, A HOME OFFICE IS INGENIOUSLY POSITIONED TO TAKE ADVANTAGE OF THE SPACE. NATURAL LIGHT FLOWS IN FROM THE ROOM'S FRENCH DOORS; AN ORIENTAL AREA RUG ON TOP OF WALL-TO-WALL CARPETING SETS THE SPACE APART; AND THE COCKPITLIKE DESIGN OF THE DESK, WHICH WRAPS AROUND THE WORK AREA, KEEPS EVERYTHING WITHIN EASY REACH AND GIVES THE SPACE A MEASURE OF PRIVACY.

office equipment companies are beginning to produce beautifully designed scaled-down pieces that work splendidly in home-based settings. In fact, the trend to work out of a home office is fueling a whole new market in the furniture industry—one that emphasizes pieces that can accommodate an ever-changing array of equipment and an always growing array of needs. But comfort, form, and function must converge in these pieces; workers want and need attractive furnishings that will not only transform areas of their homes into environments conducive to their particular working habits, but will also meet their aesthetic tastes.

Creating the right kind of home office is a fundamental need that every home worker must meet. Anyone can pack all sorts of sophisticated equipment into a space, but making that space efficient and effective, as well as comfortable and appealing, is truly a challenge, as is finding an appropriate

Above: SERENITY REIGNS SUPREME IN THIS TRANQUIL SETTING, THANKS TO ITS STREAMLINED DESIGN. THE ELEVATED BOOKSHELF IS AN UNUSUAL YET EFFECTIVE DEVICE THAT GIVES THE ROOM BROADER PROPORTIONS AND HELPS EVOKE AN ORIENTAL OVERTONE IN THE SPACE. GLOSSY BLACK WORK SURFACES, DARK RED WOOD VENEERS, AND COOL GRAY-PAINTED WALLS, ALONG WITH THE IMMACULATE STATE OF THE ENTIRE OFFICE SETUP, CONTRIBUTE TO THIS AURA.

space in the first place. Since the equipment available is incredibly compact, the options are seemingly endless. Closets, bookcases, and even kitchen crannies are all contenders as work spaces, and can be just as vital as a whole spare room. And issues such as seating, storage, lighting, and layout must be taken into account. Some home offices are merely attempts to duplicate a corporate setting in a spare room furnished with massive desks, file cabinets, and credenzas. But more often than not, people choose to inject their home offices with personality and individual style.

Some people consult designers, while others do it on their own. In either case, the home worker's tastes and preferences are extremely important in the process of creating this sort of office, for such a work space is first and foremost a part of the home. The decor that the individual selects must ultimately be integrated into his or her abode.

Above: AN INTERESTING HOME OFFICE THAT HAS LOADS OF STYLE CAN EASILY BE CREATED WITH THE RIGHT KIND OF FURNISHINGS. HERE, PIECES THAT ARE PRIME EXAMPLES OF CONTEMPORARY DESIGN PROVIDE AN EFFECTIVE FOUNDATION FOR A REMARKABLY APPOINTED WORK SPACE. EVERYTHING ABOUT THIS DESK AND COMPACT CREDENZA POINTS TO VERSATILITY, SUCH AS FOLDOUT EXTENSIONS ON THE WORK SURFACES AND CASTERS ON THE LEGS. FURNISHINGS OF THIS ILK CAN BE USED IN ANY SETTING TO CARVE OUT AN EXCEPTIONAL WORK ENVIRONMENT IN A SMALL AMOUNT OF SPACE.

Fashioned for Function

Most home offices start out very different from the way they end up. A simple desk with a phone and computer may be all that is needed to get going. Then, perhaps, a printer and photocopier are added to the ensemble. Before long, files crowd the floor and supplies consume the space in a slapdash fashion.

Offices need to be highly functional domains, so a lot of thought must be given to the way the space is used and what it contains. While a bare-bones setup may serve the needs of some, a full-service spread, complete with a conference table and a work space for a coworker, may be necessary for others. But whether one employs a decorative desk or a sensible work station, the place in which work is conducted needs to be efficiently configured so that resources are kept within easy reach. Putting a file cabinet or printer at the opposite end of the room from the desk does not make sense if these pieces of equipment are used frequently.

Built-ins are one of the best ways to tailor a work space to individual needs. They are capable of everything from housing electronic equipment to storing important files to saturating a space with convenient out-of-the-way shelves. Fabricated in many materials and fashioned in dozens of different decorative styles, built-ins can be easily incorporated into any milieu. A sleek and contemporary unit may be elegant in a laminate, while a traditional-looking setup can be downright luxurious in wood.

Opposite: WITH THE HELP OF A FEW MODEST MATERIALS (SUCH AS FORMICA WORK SURFACES, PREFABRICATED WALL-HUNG SHELVES, AND FILE CABINETS) AND AN ASTUTE USE OF SPACE, THIS OFFICE WAS DESIGNED FOR BOTH APPEARANCE AND PERFORMANCE. THE MONOCHROMATIC APPROACH GIVES THE UNIT AN EXPENSIVELY ELEGANT LOOK, WHILE A FEW SIMPLE ACCESSORIES, SUCH AS WICKER CHAIRS, A WARM RED RUG, AND SOME KNICKKNACKS IN EARTHY TONES, ADD POLISH TO THE ROOM. Above: A CREATIVE APPROACH BEGOT THIS ASYMMETRICAL WALL UNIT, WHICH EFFECTIVELY ORGANIZES ITS OWNER. ODDLY SHAPED ITEMS SUCH AS ENVELOPES, CANCELED CHECKS, AND EVEN MASSIVE PHONE BOOKS ALL HAVE THEIR OWN SPECIAL SPOTS. BEST OF ALL, THIS SETUP REQUIRES A MINIMAL AMOUNT OF SPACE AND CAN WORK IN A VARIETY OF DIFFERENT SETTINGS.

Above: Wraparound built-ins rimming the perimeter of this room make the space seem larger than it actually is. The simple yet refined light-toned color scheme further opens up the room, which comfortably accommodates two spacious work stations. French doors add to the airy feeling, ushering in light from a source other than the office's single window. **Opposite:** Here, a large open room has been partitioned by a striking system of shelves. As a result, an intimate work space with an efficient galley-style layout has been created. The dynamic shade of yellow that lines the shelves energizes the area, preventing it from appearing too sterile.

Opposite: FRONTED WITH LUXURIOUS WOOD VENEERS, THIS UNIT IS SET OFF FROM THE REST OF THE WHITE ROOM AND THEREBY IMBUED WITH AN AIR OF IMPORTANCE. OVERHEAD CABINETS PROVIDE EXTRA STORAGE THAT CAN BE USED FOR EITHER WORK-RELATED RECORDS OR PERSONAL EFFECTS, SUCH AS OUT-OF-SEASON CLOTHING. **Below:** JUST OVER TWO FEET (60CM) DEEP, THIS SPACE WAS CHOPPED OFF A HALLWAY AND TURNED INTO AN OFFICE WITH THE HELP OF A SIMPLE DARK GLASS PARTITION. THE UTILITARIAN CORK-COVERED WALL AND IMAGINATIVE STEPPED-UP WOODEN WORK SURFACE ARE AT THE SAME TIME EXTREMELY BASIC AND INVENTIVELY BOLD, ALLOWING THE MINUTE SETUP TO MAKE A MAJOR IMPACT.

Above: GIVEN THE SPACIOUS NATURE OF TODAY'S WALK-IN CLOSETS, THE DECISION TO CONVERT ONE INTO A HOME OFFICE MAKES A LOT OF SENSE. HERE, A FAIRLY AMPLE CLOSET HAS BEEN COMPLETELY REDONE FOR AN ARCHITECT, WITH SHELVING AND WORK STATIONS TAKING THE PLACE OF CLOTHING RODS. SHIFTING BETWEEN THE DRAFTING TABLE AND THE COMPUTER IS BOTH COMFORTABLE AND QUICK WITH THE HELP OF A CHAIR ON WHEELS, AND SLIDING PARTITIONS ARE OUTFITTED WITH TRANSLUCENT GLASS SO THAT THEY CONTINUE TO ALLOW LIGHT INTO THE SPACE WHEN THE DOORS ARE CLOSED, WHILE AT THE SAME TIME PRESERVING A DEGREE OF PRIVACY.

Below: BUILT-INS CAN BE SLEEK, HIGHLY STYLED, AND SOPHISTICATED WITHOUT BEING SPECIFICALLY CONTEMPORARY. ELEMENTS OF COLONIAL STYLING AND THE WARM BURNISHED HUE OF WOOD GIVE THIS ROOM A COUNTRY DEMEANOR, EVEN THOUGH IT INCORPORATES THOROUGHLY UP-TO-DATE DETAILS SUCH AS FORMICA COUNTERTOPS. THE WINDSOR ROCKERS AND CHAIR REINFORCE THE ROOM'S PERIOD DECOR. **Opposite:** IT TOOK NOTHING MORE THAN A FEW PLANKS OF WOOD TO FABRICATE THIS SIMPLE OFFICE, BUT THE EFFECT IS STRIKING THANKS TO THE EXCEPTIONAL BEAUTY OF THE SETTING. THE VIEW MAKES A MAGNIFICENT BACKDROP; THE LOCATION OFFERS AN ABUNDANCE OF NATURAL LIGHT; AND THE MINIMAL—BUT EFFECTIVE—SETUP ALLOWS THE SPECTACULAR ARCHITECTURAL DETAILING OF THE STRUCTURE TO SHINE THROUGH. THE OFFICE'S RICH WOOD BLENDS IN SPLENDIDLY WITH THE WOODSY OUTDOOR SURROUNDINGS THAT ARE SO PREVALENT THANKS TO THE IMMENSE WINDOWS.

Above: THIS BUILT-IN UNIT HAS BEEN ARTFULLY CONSTRUCTED TO HOLD A WIDE VARIETY OF OFFICE NECESSITIES. IT NOT ONLY INCORPORATES A CABINET THAT STORES LEGAL-SIZE HANGING FILES AND A COMPUTER DRIVE INVENTIVELY PLACED VERTICALLY, BUT IT ALSO MAKES THE MOST OF A SHALLOW ALCOVE THAT WAS FORMERLY A CLOSET. NOW A BOOKCASE, THIS NOOK HAS A GLASSED-IN TOP THAT KEEPS BOOKS DUST-FREE, WHILE THE OPEN BOTTOM LEAVES THE OCCUPANT A LITTLE EXTRA LEG ROOM.

Opposite: IN THIS FAMILY ROOM, A SET OF BUILT-IN SHELVES HAS BEEN REVAMPED WITH THE SIMPLE ADDITION OF A FILE CABINET, A CHAIR, AND SOME WOODEN PLANKS. THE PALE OFF-WHITE HUE OF THE WALLS AND THE LIGHT SHADE OF WOOD SET THE PERFECT TONE FOR THE ROOM, WHICH OPENS OUT ONTO A REFRESHING TERRACE WITH A BREATHTAKING VIEW OF THE OCEAN. THE USE OF A BEIGE WICKER WASTEPAPER BASKET, WHICH FURTHER COMPLEMENTS THE ROOM'S AIRY TONE, SHOWS HOW EVEN THE SMALLEST OFFICE ACCOUTREMENTS CAN BE INCORPORATED TO COORDINATE WITH THE OVERALL DECOR. **Below:** EVEN THOUGH THIS BALCONY OFF A STAIRWELL IS A PUBLIC AREA OF THE HOME, IT EFFECTIVELY HOUSES A PRODUCTIVE HOME OFFICE. FACING AWAY FROM THE CONVERSATIONAL SEATING AREA, THE ACTUAL WORK SPACE IS SITUATED COMFORTABLY OUT OF RANGE OF THE SPACE'S TRAFFIC PATTERNS. THE LIGHT NATURAL WOOD USED FOR THE DESK AREA, ALONG WITH THE DEEP GREEN HUE OF THE SURROUNDING WALL, VISUALLY DISTINGUISHES THE WORK SPACE FROM THE REST OF THE WHITE BALCONY. UNLIKE THE SEATING AREA, WHICH IS ILLUMINATED BY SOOTHING SOFT WHITE LIGHT, THE DESK AREA HAS FLUORESCENT LIGHTING, WHICH FURTHER SEPARATES THE WORK SPACE FROM THE REST OF THE ROOM.

Above: THIS RELATIVELY SPACIOUS AND ELEGANTLY NEUTRAL OFFICE WASHED IN A WARM OFF-WHITE HUE HAS BEEN CLEVERLY CARVED OUT OF A MODESTLY SIZED SPACE. WRAPPING AROUND A NARROW CORNER, THE BUILT-IN WORK SURFACE IS ABLE TO ACCOMMODATE A COMPUTER AND SEPARATE WORK STATION, WHILE A CHAIR ON WHEELS CAN BE ROLLED BETWEEN THESE TWO DESK AREAS. CAREFULLY PLANNED SHELVES MOUNTED ABOVE THE WORK SURFACE HARBOR ENOUGH NOOKS AND CRANNIES TO PLACE AN ASSORTMENT OF WORKING MATERIALS WITHIN EASY REACH.

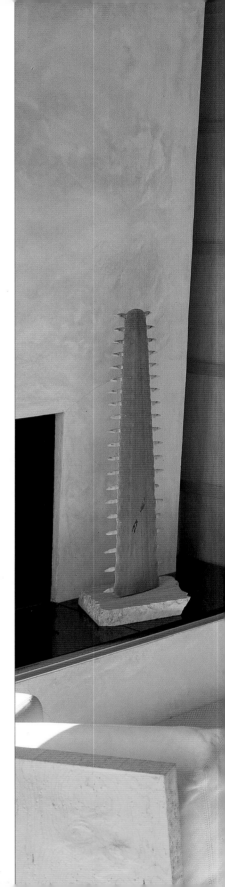

Right: THIS FORMER BAR AREA OVERLOOKING A STUNNING LIVING ROOM WAS INGENIOUSLY CONVERTED INTO A STYLISH, COMPACT HOME OFFICE. THE HANDSOME GRANITE COUNTERTOP IS JUST AS APPROPRIATE FOR WORKING AS IT IS FOR EATING AND DRINKING, AND THE AMPLE STORAGE SPACE IN THE GALLEYLIKE SETUP IS SUPPLEMENTED BY SHELVES JUST OUTSIDE ITS ENTRANCE. A WHIMSICAL LAMP AND HIGHLY STYLED STOOLS, ALL IN HUES OF BEIGE AND BLACK, SERVICE THE OFFICE AREA AND BLEND IN BEAUTIFULLY WITH THE LIVING ROOM'S WARM CONTEMPORARY FURNISHINGS.

Above: USED TO ITS FULLEST POTENTIAL, EVEN A SLIVER OF SPACE CAN BE TRANSFORMED INTO A PRODUCTIVE OFFICE. HERE A SMALL YET SLEEKLY STYLED HOME OFFICE HAS BEEN SKILLFULLY TACKED ONTO THE SCANT SPACE SURROUNDING A WINDOW. THE DESK'S ELLIPTICAL SHAPE, WHICH SOFTENS THE LOOK OF THE SETUP, EXPANDS THE DEPTH OF THE WORK SURFACE AND IS ECHOED BY TWO SHELVES THAT LEND THE UNIT AN AIR OF SOPHISTICATION. ILLUMINATION IS PROVIDED BY BOTH HIDDEN RECESSED LIGHTING AND A TASK LAMP.

Below: A totally private space has been literally sliced off another room to create this quiet and secluded office, which is fully stocked with audio-visual equipment as well as traditional business supplies. The dividing wall is ingeniously fitted with an interior window, which allows illumination to flow through from the area's only source of natural light and can also be opened or closed for soundproofing and ventilation. A mirrored wall is employed to visually enlarge the bedroom that has been reduced in size on account of the office creation. **Opposite:** This charming tableau under a graceful staircase is actually an artfully arranged reading space. Although the choice of accessories seems predicated by form, they are all actually quite functional. The elegant table that serves as a desk provides an adequate work surface; a sideboard abutting the piece has several ample drawers for storage; and a funky halogen fixture is a superior source of light. Plus, a large shelving unit adjacent to the area offers plentiful storage for periodicals.

Above: Situated on a balcony that offers a lovely view of the dining room below, this novel home office provides plenty of room for spreading out papers and storing supplies without eating up much of the home's functional space. Light floods the area thanks to an arresting skylight and a matching glass-paneled wall, making this office a cheerful, uplifting place in which to work. These panels are echoed by a row of glass blocks that adds a touch of elegance as well as prevents objects from plummeting off the balcony's edge.

DOUBLE-DUTY SPACES

"A room of one's own," which the British author Virginia Woolf found to be a crucial prerequisite for creativity, is ideal for anyone working out of the home. But many of us do not have the luxury of possessing an entire room that can be devoted solely to our work.

Hence, the rise of the double-duty room: an area decidedly devoted to two or more endeavors. Although the notion of establishing a work space in a multipurpose room is definitely not new, this type of office is now being designed far more imaginatively and effectively than ever before. A good deal of deliberation is going into the process, and the spaces that are emerging reflect both practical needs and decorative tastes. Because these offices are configured in shared spaces, close attention is focused upon visually integrating the work area with the surrounding decor. Office furnishings are often innovative and informal, taking their cues from the rest of the room. Shelves are turned over to objects an occupant may enjoy looking at, and artwork enlivens the walls.

Any kind of room can be mined for a home office, from a guest room to a full-service gym. But bedrooms, family rooms, and libraries seem to be the areas that are most often adapted for this purpose, as they usually harbor the largest amount of excess space.

Opposite: WITH PROPER PLANNING, A BEDROOM CAN BECOME A COMPREHENSIVE AND EFFICIENT HOME OFFICE. THE ELEMENTS USED TO CREATE THIS ROOMY WORK AREA HAVE BEEN ASTUTELY TAILORED TO MAKE THE MOST OF THE SPACE. ROUNDED CABINETS PROVIDE EXTRA DEPTH BY ENVELOPING THE AREA'S CORNERS, WHICH WOULD OTHERWISE BE DEAD SPACE. WHILE SHELVES ABOVE THE CENTER OF THE DESK HAVE BEEN RAISED TO ACCOMMODATE A COMPUTER MONITOR, THE CORNER CABINETS DROP DOWN TO FURNISH MORE ROOM FOR STORAGE. CAREFUL ATTENTION HAS ALSO BEEN DIRECTED TOWARD THE DECOR, AS EVIDENCED BY THE CREAMY TONES OF THE OFFICE, WHICH ECHO THE BEIGE ACCENTS OF THE BED AREA. Above: SIMPLE ORNAMENTAL EMBELLISHMENTS ALLOW THE CLUBBY DECORATIVE THEME OF A BEDROOM TO CARRY OVER INTO THE BUILT-IN OFFICE THAT SHARES THE SPACE. THE WORK SURFACE AND DRAWERS ARE ARTICULATED WITH DETAILING REMINISCENT OF REGENCY STYLING, WHILE THE WHOLE UNIT IS PAINTED A DEEP SHADE OF GREEN. A MAJESTIC LEATHER AND WOOD CHAIR WITH A DECIDEDLY BRITISH OVERTONE COMPLETES THE LOOK AND COORDINATES WITH THE ORNATELY CARVED MAHOGANY BED.

Above: BECAUSE DEVOTING AN ENTIRE ROOM TO A HOME OFFICE CAN BE DIFFICULT, THE OWNER OF THIS FULLY EQUIPPED YET CASUAL WORK SPACE ADDED AMENITIES THAT ALLOW IT TO FUNCTION AS A GUEST ROOM AS WELL. A COMFORTABLE SLEEPING AREA, WHICH HOUSES MUCH-NEEDED BUILT-IN STORAGE, WAS CARVED OUT OF AN ALCOVE BY TOPPING A BANK OF LOW DRAWERS WITH AN INVITING MATTRESS AND THROW PILLOWS. **Right:** A CAREFULLY EDITED MILIEU DEMANDS AN OFFICE TO MATCH. IN THIS ELEGANT BUT AUSTERE BEDROOM, ATTENTION IS IMMEDIATELY DRAWN TO THE DRAMATIC ASPECTS OF THE SPACE, SUCH AS THE HIGH CONTRAST OF THE BEIGE AND BLACK COLOR SCHEME AND THE STRIKING FRANK GEHRY BENTWOOD CHAIR. AN OFFICE THAT COMPLEMENTS, RATHER THAN COMPETES WITH, THESE COMPONENTS IS UNOBTRUSIVELY POSITIONED AT THE FAR END OF THE ROOM. THE WRAPAROUND DESK, FABRICATED FROM THE SAME MATERIALS AS THE BED AND BUILT-IN CABINETS, FEATURES THE SAME KIND OF STYLING AS THESE OTHER FURNISHINGS, WHILE THE HIGH-CONTRAST MOTIF IS CARRIED THROUGH BY THE BLACK SHELVES AND DESK CHAIR.

Opposite: A WARM, RICH CHERRY WALL UNIT, WHICH IS NEUTRAL
ENOUGH TO BLEND IN WITH PIECES FROM OTHER ERAS, SUCH
AS A MISSION ROCKER AND A VICTORIAN CLOTHES RACK, IS USED TO
OUTFIT THIS BEDROOM WITH A FUNCTIONAL WORK SPACE. THE
FURNITURE'S PHYSICAL VERSATILITY IS AN ADDED BONUS: NOTE THE
NIGHTSTAND, WHICH IS ACTUALLY A MATCHING FILE CABINET.

Below: AN UNUSUAL UNIT MODELED AFTER A TRADITIONAL PARTNERS
DESK BUT ALTERED WITH CLEVER MODIFICATIONS ALLOWS THIS
DRESSING AREA TO DOUBLE AS AN OFFICE. FLOOR-TO-CEILING MIRRORS
COVER THE DOORS TO THE CLOSET, WHICH PROVIDES STORAGE
FOR BOTH CLOTHES AND OFFICE ACCOUTREMENTS, AND VISUALLY EXPAND
THE SPACE. BUT A LOW-PILE CARPET AND A TOTAL LACK OF CLUTTER
CREATE THE OPEN AND AIRY FEELING OF THE AREA.

Above: FLANKED BY STATELY WHITE COLUMNS, THIS WORK SPACE IS
GRACED WITH A MAJESTIC, CLASSICAL AMBIENCE THAT IS REFRESHINGLY DIFFERENT
FROM THE CASUAL YET BUSY TONE OF THE FAMILY ROOM SHARING THE
AREA. NONETHELESS, THE DECOR RETAINS A SENSE OF HARMONY THANKS TO
THE EMERALD GREEN WALLS THAT ENVELOP THE ROOM.

Opposite: AN OFFICE TUCKED AWAY IN A CORNER OF A KITCHEN CAN STILL AFFORD AMPLE STORAGE. DESK DRAWERS AND A WHOLE WALL OF CABINETS ARE CONFIGURED TO LOOK LIKE KITCHEN CUPBOARDS, BUT ARE ACTUALLY A BIT DEEPER AND HIDE FILES AND WORKING MATERIALS. **Below:** FOLDING DOORS ARE USED TO CONCEAL THIS WELL-DESIGNED WORK SPACE THAT HAS BEEN CREATED OFF A KITCHEN DINING AREA. UNOBTRUSIVELY PROMOTING THE SEPARATION OF WORK AND FAMILY LIFE, THESE DOORS CAN BE CLOSED SO THAT THE KITCHEN RECLAIMS A MORE HOMEY AMBIENCE WHEN THE FAMILY IS GATHERED THERE FOR MEALS.

Above: EVEN THOUGH THIS HOME OFFICE IS NOTHING MORE THAN A WORK STATION AT ONE END OF A KITCHEN, IT IS SURPRISINGLY COMPREHENSIVE. A CREDENZA THAT RUNS FROM A BANK OF BUILT-IN KITCHEN EQUIPMENT TO THE ROOM'S FAR WALL IS FABRICATED FROM THE SAME MATERIALS AS THE "OFFICIAL" KITCHEN CABINETS, AND CONSISTS OF FILE CABINETS AND SUPPLY DRAWERS TOPPED BY A VAST WORK SURFACE. THE AREA RECEIVES AN ABUNDANCE OF NATURAL LIGHT FROM LARGE WINDOWS AND A SKYLIGHT, WHILE A BANK OF RECESSED CANISTERS PROVIDES TASK LIGHTING.

Opposite: DESPITE THE FACT THAT BASIC FURNISHINGS HAVE BEEN USED TO CONFIGURE THIS COMBINATION OFFICE/SITTING ROOM, COLOR AND TEXTURE IMBUE IT WITH A POLISHED AIR OF SOPHISTICATION. THE CARPETING, WALLS, BLINDS, BUILT-IN SHELVES, AND DESK ARE ALL EXECUTED IN THE SAME SUBTLE, WARM TONES, AND A RICH VELVETEEN GIVES THE SLEEPER SOFA A MEASURE OF OPULENCE. THE OVERALL EFFECT IS ANYTHING BUT ORDINARY.

Above: OPTIMAL USE IS MADE OF A CORNER IN THIS FAMILY ROOM: A DRAFTING TABLE IS SITUATED NEXT TO THE SOURCE OF NATURAL LIGHT; A DESK IS PLACED IN A RECESSED ALCOVE; AND A SET OF BUILT-IN SHELVES IS POSITIONED IN BETWEEN TO ALLOW EASY ACCESS FROM EITHER WORK STATION. WORKS OF ART INTERSPERSED IN THIS TINY AREA, WHICH IS BUT A SMALL PART OF THE ROOM, IMPART IT WITH SIGNIFICANCE AND DRAMA, WHILE A UNIQUE TWO-TONE MOLDING TREATMENT THAT RIMS THE ROOM'S PERIMETER UNIFIES THE OFFICE WITH THE REST OF THE SPACE.

Left: SITUATED AT ONE END OF A FAMILY ROOM, THIS HOME OFFICE HAS EFFECTIVELY BEEN SET APART FROM THE REST OF THE SPACE WITH THE HELP OF A WRAPAROUND WORK SURFACE—FORMED BY A STRATEGIC CONFIGURATION OF MIX-AND-MATCH PIECES—THAT ACTS AS A DIVIDER. COMFORTABLE ARMCHAIRS FACE INWARD TOWARD THE DESK, FURTHER IMBUING THE OFFICE AREA WITH INTIMACY. **Above:** THE OFFICELIKE CHORES OF EVERYDAY LIFE, SUCH AS PAYING BILLS OR WRITING LETTERS, CAN BE STREAMLINED BY HAVING A SPECIAL WORK SPACE. HERE, A CORNER OF A FORMAL LIBRARY IS DEVOTED TO THESE NECESSARY TASKS WITH THE HELP OF A FOLDING SCREEN THAT IS CLEVERLY USED TO DISPLAY INCOMING CORRESPONDENCE AND IMPORTANT REMINDERS. WHILE THESE NOTES REMAIN NEATLY OUT OF SIGHT FROM OTHER VANTAGE POINTS IN THE ROOM, THEY ARE HIGHLY VISIBLE AT THE DESK. FURTHERMORE, THIS NOVEL USE OF THE SCREEN FREES UP DRAWER SPACE FOR OFFICE SUPPLIES AND DOCUMENTS OF A MORE PRIVATE NATURE.

Right: Integrating a functional working area into an elegant milieu can often be challenging. Here, an exquisite mahogany table, which picks up the wood of the fireplace directly opposite, doubles as a desk in a sophisticated but eclectic living room. Stacks of books interspersed in the space create a slightly nonchalant mood.

Above: There is room for work and play in this deftly arranged space, which serves as an office and exercise center for a couple. An alcove off the room's entrance incorporates a desk, shelves, and file cabinets, and is cleverly enlarged with the adroit use of a floor-to-ceiling mirror and recessed lighting. Another desk hems in the work area and separates it from the gym, creating an informal but effective barrier that enhances the performance of the space.

TRADITIONALLY SPEAKING

The very notion of a traditional home office conjures up images of a British men's club, replete with sumptuous paneling, soothing dark hues, and pieces upholstered in leather. But the word "traditional" embraces many different styles, all connected by the fact that they have achieved historical acceptance and renown.

Rooms that are referred to as "traditional" fill us with a certain response, for they embrace a decor that we find familiar. The furnishings are either old or made to look that way, and they remind us of days gone by. Yet despite this common thread, they come in an amazingly wide variety of incarnations.

An office brimming with neoclassical styling can be just as traditional as one that is quintessentially British club—as can a Victorian vista that is crammed with extravagant Baroque pickings. Moreover, any of these various styles can be combined yet still evoke a mood that seems true to a specific tradition.

Thus, the traditional home office of today may be filled with a combination of furnishings that are Colonial, Shaker, or Federal in form, but have an all-American historical appeal. Or pieces that are Empire, Regency, and Biedermeier in origin can be used to make a room seem decidedly European. Even styles from the late nineteenth and twentieth centuries, such as Victorian, Arts and Crafts, and Mission, as well as those derived from ethnic origins, are eligible for the mix. What matters is mood rather than strict adherence to a style's purity.

Opposite: KNOTTY PINE PANELING DELINEATED WITH FEDERAL STYLING IMPARTS A SENSE OF HISTORY TO THIS HANDSOME ROOM THAT IS THE EPITOME OF A TRADITIONAL HOME OFFICE. A COZY SITTING AREA OVERLOOKING AN INVITING FIREPLACE MAKES AN IDEAL SPOT FOR WORKING WITH CLIENTS OR RELAXING. Above: SUMPTUOUS TUFTED LEATHER CHAIRS AND A DARK STAINED WOODEN DESK LEND AN AIR OF AUTHORITY TO THIS COMFORTABLE HOME OFFICE. BUT FLORAL-PATTERNED DRAPES, AN ABUNDANCE OF GREENERY, AND THE GOLDEN HUE OF THE OAK WAINSCOTING AND WALL UNIT LIVEN UP THE SPACE, GIVING IT A WELCOMING AND REASSURING FEEL. PRIZED POSSESSIONS, INCLUDING AN ANTIQUE GLOBE AND AN OLD-FASHIONED TYPEWRITER, ADORN THE ROOM AND CONTRIBUTE TO THE TRADITIONAL TONE.

Opposite: THE QUINTESSENTIAL CLUB LOOK IS RELATIVELY EASY TO ACHIEVE IN AN OFFICE, EVEN ONE WITHOUT PANELING. UPHOLSTERED PIECES COVERED IN BOLD PATTERNS OR COLORS, SIMPLE TRADITIONAL FURNISHINGS FABRICATED IN DARK WOODS, AND VIVID, FLORAL AREA CARPETS OVER WOOD FLOORS ARE ALL DECORATIVE DEVICES THAT DO THE TRICK. SHELVES AND WALLS PAINTED IN STRONG, DARK HUES FURTHER IMBUE THE ROOM WITH INTENSITY. HERE, AN ELABORATE THREE-TIER CANOPIED WINDOW TREATMENT THAT IMMEDIATELY ENGAGES THE EYE ADDS EVEN MORE DRAMA AND DECORUM TO THE ROOM.

Above: ALTHOUGH THE OVERALL EFFECT OF THIS CHARMING HOME OFFICE IS "COUNTRY MANOR QUAINT," THE PIECES USED TO ACHIEVE THIS LOOK ARE ACTUALLY QUITE SOPHISTICATED AND ECLECTIC. A FRENCH ARMCHAIR MANS AN EMPIRE DESK; BIEDERMEIER FRUITWOOD CHAIRS SURROUND AN EMPIRE TABLE; AND A QUEEN ANNE WING CHAIR FLANKS SHELVES LADEN WITH BOOKS. THESE FURNISHINGS PROVIDE SPECIFIC AREAS FOR WORKING, MEETING, AND READING, WHILE DECORATIVE TOUCHES, INCLUDING FLORAL DRAPES, BEAUTIFUL TEAL WALLS, ORIENTAL CARPETS, AND A RUSTIC COFFERED CEILING, LULL ONE INTO SEEING THE SPACE IN A FAR MORE CASUAL LIGHT.

Above: THIS VARIATION ON THE CLUB THEME FOLLOWS ALL THE RULES, WITH THE EXCEPTION OF ITS INTERESTING WALL TREATMENT. ALTHOUGH PANELING IS USED ON THE BUILT-IN SHELVES AND ON MOST OF THE WALLS, THE AREA SANDWICHED BETWEEN THE MOLDING AND CEILING IS FINISHED OFF WITH PATTERNED WALLPAPER DISPLAYING DEEP SHADES OF BLUE AND RED THAT COORDINATE WITH THE UPHOLSTERED ARMCHAIR, THE AREA RUG, AND EVEN THE LAMP SHADES. TO GIVE THE ROOM ADDED DEPTH, THE CEILING HAS BEEN PAINTED A SOFT SHADE OF BROWN THAT IS SUBSTANTIALLY LIGHTER THAN THE OTHER COLORS EMPLOYED IN THE DECOR.

Opposite: BLENDING IN BEAUTIFULLY WITH A VARIETY OF DIVERSE FURNISHINGS AND STRONG ARCHITECTURAL COMPONENTS, A PARTNERS DESK WITH COLONIAL STYLING IS THE FOCAL POINT OF THIS RELATIVELY RELAXED OFFICE SPACE. THE PLACEMENT OF THE DESK IS ASTUTE, ALLOWING THE OCCUPANTS OF THE OFFICE EASY ACCESS TO THE BUILT-IN SHELVES. **Above:** TWO SIGNIFICANT STYLES ARE BLENDED SKILLFULLY AND SEAMLESSLY IN THIS FORMAL LIBRARY AND OFFICE SPACE WITH STUNNING RESULTS. THE NEOCLASSICAL ARCHITECTURAL DETAILS OF THE ROOM, SUCH AS THE DORIC COLUMNS AND THE GOUGEWORK PATTERN IN THE WAINSCOTING, ARE PURE EMPIRE, WHILE THE FURNISHINGS AND ACCESSORIES ARE PERFECT EXAMPLES OF ARTS AND CRAFTS DESIGN. THE SUCCESS OF THE DECOR IS OWED TO THE SIMPLICITY OF THE REST OF ITS EFFECTS, SUCH AS THE USE OF RECESSED LIGHTING INSTEAD OF FIXTURES AND SUBTLE MINIBLINDS INSTEAD OF FULL-BLOWN WINDOW TREATMENTS.

Below: THE QUAINT COLONIAL APPEAL OF THE DECOR EFFECTIVELY MASKS THE HIGHLY PRODUCTIVE NATURE OF THIS HOME OFFICE. A BANK OF BUILT-IN CABINETS EMBELLISHED WITH PERIOD TRIM INCORPORATES A DESK, LEAVING THE CENTER OF THE ROOM FREE FOR A LARGE PEDESTAL TABLE THAT CAN BE USED FOR MEETINGS OR COMMUNAL PROJECTS. FETCHING ACCENTS, SUCH AS DEEPLY HUED WALLS AND TIEBACK DRAPES, HELP COMPLETE THE CHARMING PICTURE.

Above: ONE OF THE BENEFITS OF WORKING AT HOME IS TAKING ADVANTAGE OF THE ENVIRONMENT'S ASSETS. HERE, A SECTION OF AN UNUSUALLY LARGE GREAT ROOM THAT BORDERS A BEAUTIFUL BACKYARD HAS BEEN CONVERTED INTO A PLEASANT HOME OFFICE THAT MAKES THE MOST OF THE HOME'S INTERIOR AND EXTERIOR ATTRIBUTES. A MASSIVE SHELVING UNIT TOPPED WITH TRIM THAT EMULATES MOLDING IS USED TO DEFINE THE OFFICE, WHILE DESKS DETAILED WITH TOUCHES OF CLASSICAL STYLING ARE PLACED END-TO-END TO FACE THE BACKYARD.

Opposite: A COMPROMISE WAS REACHED IN THIS TASTEFUL ROOM THAT TREADS A FINE LINE BETWEEN THE SEXES. THE IMPOSING TUFTED LEATHER SOFA IS ALL MALE, WHILE THE ELEGANT QUEEN ANNE DESK HAS A FAR MORE FEMININE SILHOUETTE. THE SPARE WHITE BUILT-INS AND PALE BLUE WALLS CREATE A NEUTRAL BACKDROP, WHICH IS ACCENTED BY ARTIFACTS THAT OFFER A BALANCE, SUCH AS HANDSOME ANTIQUE LEATHER-BOUND BOOKS AND FINE MEDITERRANEAN POTTERY.

Opposite: In this striking office, elegance and grandeur are balanced by eclectic abandon, illustrating that traditional trappings are not always tame. Federal and Empire styling, with their neoclassical motifs, are still the prevalent influences employed here, evident in the architectural elements and most of the furnishings. But this office is also rife with fantastic oddities that add a whimsical spirit to the space. Pieces such as a fanciful horn chair, a spectacular chandelier, and a hand-painted turn-of-the-century lamp immediately grab the eye and set a new standard for the room.

Above: Color and tone are deftly used in this exquisite setting to both enrich and offset the effects of the dark woods. Beautiful antique leather books are bound in luxuriant shades of black, red, brown, and green, and are heavily embossed with radiant gold leaf, a color scheme that is echoed throughout the room. The Empire armchair, the Directoire desk, an elegant oil, an opulent throw, and even a stunning topiary pot are all gilt-encrusted, gleaming seductively in the setting. **Right:** The ambience inspired by a wild animal theme can be cunningly called up without actually displaying anything that has been stuffed. Here, an inventive window treatment tricks the eye by creating the image of a powerful leopard's head, while pieces with leopard patterning are skillfully interspersed throughout the space. The rest of the room's appointments are tinged with tints of honey and accented with touches of black, further reinforcing the motif.

Opposite: THIS UNIQUE WORK SPACE IS THE PERFECT HAVEN FOR AN ADMIRER OF REGENCY AND EMPIRE STYLING. THE BREATHTAKING BEAUTY OF A NEOCLASSICAL MOSAIC FLOOR, COUPLED WITH A COMFORTABLY CUSHIONED SEATING AREA CARVED OUT OF A SECLUDED CORNER, MAKES THE SPACE ENTICING, WHILE PERIOD FURNISHINGS COMPLETE THE PRETTY PICTURE. BUT THE EARTHY TONES OF THE TILE, COUPLED WITH THE COOL GREEN HUE ON THE WALLS, MAKES THE SPACE EXCEPTIONALLY CAPTIVATING.

Above: A CONTEMPORARY DWELLING CAN EASILY HARBOR A TRADITIONAL OFFICE WITH THE HELP OF THE RIGHT DECORATIVE DEVICES. GIVEN THE MODERNIST OVERTONES EVIDENT IN THE ARCHITECTURE, JAPONAISERIE STYLING MAKES A LOT OF SENSE FOR THIS ABODE. ALTHOUGH IT NEVER REACHED THE HEIGHTS OF CHINOISERIE, A CONSIDERABLE AMOUNT OF FURNITURE OF THIS ILK WAS STILL BEING MADE DURING THE NINETEENTH CENTURY. THIS DESK IS CLEARLY OF THAT PERIOD AND IS PERFECTLY PAIRED WITH FRENCH EMPIRE CHAIRS. A JAPANESE SCREEN MOUNTED ON THE WALL MAKES THE ORIENTAL EFFECT EVEN MORE PRONOUNCED.

Above: TWO-PERSON OFFICES ARE OFTEN DIFFICULT TO DESIGN, BUT THE PARTNERS DESK PROVIDES AN ENGAGING AND EQUITABLE WAY TO SHARE SPACE. PLUS, IT CAN BE FOUND, OR FABRICATED, IN VIRTUALLY EVERY VARIATION, SO IT CAN BE INTEGRATED INTO ANY DECOR. HERE, AN EXQUISITE FEDERAL-STYLE VERSION IS THE CENTERPIECE OF A CAREFULLY BALANCED ROOM. AN EMPIRE OTTOMAN AND MATCHING CHAIRS MINGLE HARMONIOUSLY WITH THE CONTEMPORARY PIECES IN THE SETTING, THANKS TO THE SOPHISTICATED USE OF TEXTURE AND HUE IN THE CARPET AND FABRICS OUTFITTING THE ROOM.

Right: AN ECLECTIC BLEND OF FURNISHINGS FROM MANY ERAS CAN STILL IMPART A TRADITIONAL EFFECT. HERE, AN ATYPICAL MÉLANGE THAT MAKES THE MOST OF ANTIQUES WORKS AS A SUCCESSFUL DECOR BECAUSE ALL THE PIECES ARE RELAXED AND EARTHY, RATHER THAN ELEGANT AND REFINED. A VICTORIAN REPRODUCTION OF A LOUIS XVI ARMCHAIR AND A DESK WITH QUEEN ANNE STYLING ARE EQUALLY AT HOME WITH A MACHINE-AGE METAL TYPING CHAIR AND A WICKER AND BAMBOO ARMOIRE. THE NEUTRAL CREAM-COLORED BACKDROP ALSO CONTRIBUTES TO THE SUCCESS OF THE MILIEU, WHICH MANAGES TO ACCOMMODATE ALL SORTS OF HIGH-TECH EQUIPMENT INCONSPICUOUSLY.

Left: REGAL PIECES OF PURE AMERICAN VICTORIANA ARE THE ULTIMATE IN TURN-OF-THE-CENTUTY STYLING. ALTHOUGH THESE PIECES DO NOT APPEAR IN A PERIOD SETTING, THEIR STRIKING PRESENCE GIVES THIS OFFICE A TRADITIONAL AIR. DEVOID OF ARCHITECTURAL DETAILING, THE EXPANSIVE ALL-WHITE ROOM ALLOWS THE BEAUTY OF EACH PIECE TO SHINE THROUGH.

Above: FORM MEETS FUNCTION IN THIS COMPACT CORNER WALL UNIT THAT EMBRACES PERIOD DESIGN. A COUNTRY THEME, WHICH BEGINS WITH THE PANELING AND WAINSCOTING OF THE ROOM, IS FINISHED OFF BY FABRICATING THE WALL UNIT FROM THE SAME KNOTTY PINE. BUT IT IS THE BURNISHED WOOD RATHER THAN PRONOUNCED ARCHITECTURAL DETAILING THAT GIVES THE UNIT, WHICH IS RELATIVELY UNEMBELLISHED, ITS DECORATIVE FLAIR.

CONTEMPORARY LINES

Sleek designs, gleaming surfaces, and basic, elementary lines are all characteristics that come to mind when talking about contemporary design. But the breadth of this decor is actually quite immense, encompassing far more than the simple traits we normally attribute to it. While a home office with contemporary styling can be stark and pristine, it can just as easily be warm and elegant, even whimsical.

Contemporary merely means "in the style of our times," and the furnishings that are being made today take their cues from a broad spectrum of influences. Modernism, the pivotal architectural style created just before World War I, came to embody "all things contemporary" by inspiring a pared-down approach to design. But it actually paved the way for many types of decor that have evolved since that time, which embrace—yet expand upon—the style's spare, refined lines.

Today it is rare to find a home entirely given over to any singular period of design. We pick and choose furnishings with little regard for a specific style, and eclectic blends that incorporate "a bit of this and some of that" seem to be the order of the day. So when it comes to contemporary design, there are no set rules. Sleekly styled furnishings can set a contemporary tone, or pieces from various periods and cultures can be used together in a groundbreaking way. Although the spectrum of "contemporary" design is quite wide, the overall look is essentially fresh and new.

Opposite: THROUGH THE SKILLFUL USE OF CONTRAST AND COLOR, THIS HIGHLY STYLED WORK SPACE PRODUCES A DYNAMIC EFFECT. WHITE TILES AND A SOFT GRAY HUE DEFINE THE WORK STATION'S BOUNDARIES, BUT AT THE SAME TIME BLEND IN WITH THE OTHER FURNISHINGS IN THE LARGE ROOM. WHIMSICAL ELEMENTS, SUCH AS A BRIGHT RED CHAIR AND A SEMICIRCULAR DESK, ARE IMAGINATIVE TOUCHES THAT ENHANCE RATHER THAN OVERWHELM THE DECOR. **Above:** THE SIMPLICITY OF THIS CONTEMPORARY OFFICE BELIES ITS ELEGANCE, WHICH IS EVIDENT IN THE UNDERSTATED BUT SUMPTUOUS PIECES USED TO APPOINT THE ROOM. THE BUILT-INS AND SOFA ARE REFINED BUT EXTREMELY SPARE, MAKING THEM PERFECT FOILS FOR THE MODERNIST TABLES AND ELOQUENT MIES VAN DER ROHE CHAIR.

Opposite: EVERYTHING IS SHARED EQUALLY IN THIS TWO-PERSON SPACE, THANKS TO THE PERFECT SYMMETRY OF THE DESK, SHELVES, AND STORAGE CABINETS. THE DRAMATIC WORK SURFACE IS AN INVENTIVE INTERPRETATION OF A PARTNERS DESK, WITH AN INGENIOUS INSET AT ONE END THAT CAN ACCOMMODATE ANOTHER CHAIR OR TWO FOR MEETINGS. WITH ITS VIBRANT GREEN HUE, THIS HIGHLY USEFUL LEDGE ALSO SERVES AS AN ENGAGING DECORATIVE ACCENT THAT LIVENS UP THE ROOM, MAKING IT A BRIGHTER, MORE PLEASANT ENVIRONMENT IN WHICH TO WORK. COORDINATING GREEN-TINTED GLASS PROVIDES AN ADDITIONAL SPLASH OF COLOR AND HIDES UNATTRACTIVE OFFICE SUPPLIES.

Above: THOUGH THIS HOME OFFICE IS ALMOST ENTIRELY PURE WHITE, IT IS ANYTHING BUT PRISSY AND IMPRACTICAL. THE COLOR CREATES A SLEEK LOOK, STREAMLINING THE VARIED AND POWERFUL ARCHITECTURAL COMPONENTS OF THE ROOM. NOW THE COMPLEX GEOMETRY OF THE WOOD JOIST CEILING SUBTLY BLENDS IN WITH THE SOFFIT USED FOR RECESSED LIGHTING, WHILE A HANDSOME BUT PROMINENT HEARTH IS TURNED INTO A GRACEFUL FOCAL POINT FOR THE ROOM.

Opposite: WHILE AN EXPANSE OF GLASS USUALLY EMPHASIZES THE ENVIRONMENT OUTDOORS, THE OBVIOUS COMFORT AND REFINEMENT OF THIS ROOM DRAWS THE EYE BACK INSIDE. A TASTEFUL BLEND OF CLASSICALLY STYLED YET CONTEMPORARY PIECES GIVES THE ROOM A WARM AND RESTFUL AIR. **Right:** THOUGH A SOOTHING PALETTE OF EARTH TONES MAKES THIS OFFICE SEEM SUBDUED, IT IS ACTUALLY QUITE UNCONVENTIONAL. SINGULAR PIECES OF FURNITURE, SUCH AS A FUNKY SET OF SUITCASES TURNED INTO A STORAGE CHEST, BRING ORIGINALITY AND WIT TO THIS INVENTIVE CONTEMPORARY SPACE. A WALL UNIT AND CHAIR SEEM MORE STANDARD AT FIRST GLANCE, BUT ACTUALLY ONLY EMULATE MORE TRADITIONAL DESIGNS. THE CHAIR MERELY INCORPORATES TOUCHES OF CLASSICAL STYLING, WHILE THE LINES OF THE CANTILEVERED SHELVES ARE UNDENIABLY DISTINCTIVE.

Below: THE ARCHITECTURAL STRUCTURE OF A ROOM CAN BECOME AN INTEGRAL ASPECT OF ITS DESIGN, AS EVIDENCED BY THIS SPECTACULAR HOME OFFICE. HERE, THE SLANTED CEILING OF AN ATTIC SERVES AS A SOLID ANCHOR FOR A BUILT-IN UNIT THAT AFFORDS THE AREA PLENTY OF STORAGE AND AN INGENIOUS TWO-PERSON WORK SURFACE. CABINETS AND DRAWERS ARE CARVED OUT OF THE SNUG CAVITY CREATED BY THE PITCH OF THE CEILING, WHICH WOULD NORMALLY BE DEAD SPACE. THE SUBDUED TONES OF THE "TWO-TIERED" FLOOR TREATMENT WORK WELL WITH THE SIMPLE WHITES AND BLACKS EMPLOYED IN THE REST OF THE ROOM. **Opposite:** BASIC FURNISHINGS BECOME ENGAGING AND BOLD WITH THE RIGHT KIND OF ACCESSORIES TO ACCENTUATE THEM. HERE, PLAIN CONTEMPORARY PIECES WITH BLACK WOOD VENEERS RECEIVE CHARACTER FROM AN ANTIQUE DRESS FORM, FRESH FLOWERS, AND A WARM WOODEN DESK CHAIR WITH VINTAGE STYLING. INTERESTING LIGHTING ALSO JAZZES UP THE SPACE: A SLEEK TASK LAMP IS FOCUSED ON THE DESKTOP, WHILE A SCULPTURAL SPOTLIGHT ILLUMINATES THE REST OF THE ROOM.

Above: BLACK, THE COLOR SYMBOLICALLY ASSOCIATED WITH "THE ABSOLUTE," MAKES AN UNEQUIVOCAL IMPRESSION IN A ROOM. THIS STRIKING OFFICE EXUDES STRENGTH AND OFFERS AN EXTREMELY EFFICIENT ENVIRONMENT. ITS RESOURCEFUL FLOOR PLAN MAKES THE MOST OF EVERY SQUARE FOOT, WHILE THE SLEEK, DARK APPOINTMENTS SET A COMMANDING TONE.

Left: IF BUILT-INS ARE OUT OF THE QUESTION, SIMPLE MODULAR UNITS CAN BE USED TO CREATE A CLEAN, CONTEMPORARY WORK SPACE IN ANY ROOM. THE UP-TO-DATE DESIGN OF THIS SYSTEM EASILY ACCOMMODATES COMPUTER EQUIPMENT AND TAKES ERGONOMICS INTO ACCOUNT, MAKING IT AN EFFECTIVE OPTION FOR CREATING A HOME OFFICE. PLUS, ITS NEUTRAL LINES CAN JIBE WITH A WIDE RANGE OF DECORATIVE STYLES. **Above:** FURNISHINGS WITH MODERNIST STYLING ARE USED TO DEFINE AN OFFICE IN A MIES VAN DER ROHE APARTMENT, SINCE THE SPACE HAS BEEN RESTORED TO ITS ORIGINAL STATE AND IS DEVOID OF ALL WALLS. THE SIMPLICITY OF THE SETTING, WHICH IS FURTHER AFFIRMED BY THE USE OF A NEUTRAL PALETTE AND A DISCIPLINED LACK OF ACCESSORIES, ALLOWS THE INTRINSIC BEAUTY OF THE EXQUISITELY CRAFTED WOOD PIECES TO SHINE THROUGH.

Below: A RICHLY HUED, VARIEGATED PAINT JOB ADDS WARMTH TO THE PURE CONTEMPORARY LINES OF THE PIECES IN THIS ROOM AND MAKES A MAGNIFICENT BACKDROP FOR A COLLECTION OF PRE-COLUMBIAN ARTIFACTS. THOUGH THE HEAVILY GLAZED WALLS WERE ACTUALLY INTENDED TO COORDINATE WITH THE OPULENT BIRD'S-EYE MAPLE OF THE DESK AND CREDENZA, THEY ALSO MAKE THE ROOM MUCH WARMER. LOW-VOLTAGE LIGHTING DRAWS ATTENTION TO THE MOST DRAMATIC COMPONENTS OF THE SPACE—A STUNNING SYSTEM OF CANTILEVERED GLASS SHELVES AND A SLEEK FIREPLACE. **Opposite:** THROUGH THE USE OF DYNAMIC ARCHITECTURAL COMPONENTS AND CLASSIC MODERN FURNISHINGS, THIS HUGE ATTIC HAS BEEN CONVERTED INTO A SPARE BUT FASHIONABLE HOME OFFICE. A STREAMLINED SKYLIGHT AND AN UNUSUAL PICTURE WINDOW WITH A GLASS PEDIMENT EMPHASIZE THE UNIQUE BEAUTY OF THE ROOM'S STRUCTURAL "BONES," WHILE SIMPLE BUILT-INS TEAMED WITH MARCEL BREUER'S WASSILY CHAIRS ADD A COMPLEMENTARY DECORATIVE FLAIR.

Above: CHARMING ANTIQUE PIECES LEND PANACHE TO A RELATIVELY ROUTINE SET OF PLAIN WHITE SHELVES. TOGETHER THE FURNISHINGS CREATE AN INTERESTING OFFICE AREA, WHICH STILL RETAINS A CONTEMPORARY FEEL THANKS TO THE ABUNDANT LIGHTING AND CRISP TONES OF THE SETTING.

Left: THERE ARE LESSONS TO BE LEARNED FROM AN ARCHITECT'S APPROACH TO SETTING UP A CONTEMPORARY HOME OFFICE IN A VINTAGE LOFT. AN IMMENSE DESK IS ASYMMETRICALLY ALIGNED AT ONE END OF THE EXPANSIVE SPACE, CREATING AN AVANT-GARDE YET EXTREMELY EFFICIENT LAYOUT. THANKS TO ITS POSITIONING, THE DESK PROVIDES ITS OCCUPANT WITH TWO SPECIFIC TASK AREAS. **Above:** JUST A FEW SLEEK PIECES CAN HAVE A POWERFUL EFFECT IN A HOME OFFICE. DESPITE THE PROSAIC BACKDROP OF THIS ROOM, A SCULPTURAL DESK AND DEBONAIR CHAIR ADD SPIRIT AND SPUNK TO THE SETTING. THE COOL, CLEAN HUES EMPLOYED IN THE MILIEU KEEP THE MOOD DIGNIFIED AND FOCUSED ON BUSINESS.

Above: THIS OPEN EXPANSE IN A SOARING ATTIC HAS BEEN MADE INTIMATE BY BREAKING UP THE SPACE INTO SMALLER, AND DECORATIVELY DISTINCT, SETTINGS. CAREFREE WICKER CREATES A BREEZY CORNER ON ONE SIDE OF THE ROOM, WHILE MORE TRADITIONAL TRAPPINGS ARE STRATEGICALLY ARRANGED TO CARVE OUT A SERIOUS HOME OFFICE RIGHT ALONGSIDE. **Right:** THE PROFESSIONAL LOOK OF THIS TWO-PERSON SPACE WAS ACHIEVED WITH COMMERCIAL FURNISHINGS ACCENTED BY MINIMAL BUT POWERFUL PIECES OF ART. GRASSCLOTH WALLPAPER AND MATCHSTICK BLINDS IN MELLOW TONES SOFTEN THE SPACE, WHILE EYE-CATCHING COWHIDE DESK CHAIRS ADD A FANCIFUL TOUCH.

Sources

DESIGNERS

(pages 6, 28, 34, and 62)
Herman Miller for the Home
Zeeland, MI
(800) 646-4400

(page 10)
Anne Lenox
Partners in Design
Newton Center, MA
(617) 969-3626

(page 11)
Jan Tomlinson
Trophy Club, TX
(817) 491-9628

(page 13)
Walter Chatham Architects
New York, NY
(212) 925-2202

(page 14)
Keith Hone
Pennington, NJ
(212) 513-7260

(page 18)
Cathy Morehead
   and Associates
Santa Ana, CA
(714) 542-6504

(page 20)
Mark Stumer, designer
Peter Johns, assistant designer
Mojo-Stumer Associates
Roslyn, NY
(516) 625-3344

(page 22, left)
Scott Brownell, architect
Newport Beach, CA
(714) 548-6522

(page 23)
Peter Wheeler
P.J. Wheeler and Associates
Boston, MA
(617) 426-5921

(page 25)
Audio/Video Interiors
Woodland Hills, CA
(818) 593-3923

(page 29, left)
Maxine Ordesky
Organized Designs
Beverly Hills, CA
(310) 277-0499

(page 29, right)
Charles Riley
New York, NY
(212) 286-8395

(page 30)
Anna Belle Marshall, C.K.D.
Valley Concepts and Design
Lake Forest, CA
(714) 951-7898

(page 31, left)
J.P. Franzen Associates,
   Architects
Southport, CT
(203) 259-0529

(page 31, right)
Kenneth Solomon, designer
KJS Interiors, Ltd.
Glen Head, NY
(516) 759-4500

(page 35)
Charlotte Moss, designer
Charlotte Moss & Co.
New York, NY
(212) 772-6244

(page 37)
Mariette Himes, ASID
Gomez Associates
New York, NY
(212) 288-6856

(pages 40 and 49)
Joseph L. Roman, ASID
Wainscott, NY
(516) 324-5763

(page 42)
Barbara Winslow, partner in
   charge of design
Jacobson Silverstein Winslow,
   Architects
Berkeley, CA
(510) 848-8861

(page 43)
Tim Button, designer
Stedila Design, Inc.
New York, NY
(212) 865-6611

(page 47)
Vince Lattuca
New York, NY
(212) 758-2720

(page 48)
Gail Green Interior Design
New York, NY
(212) 980-1098

(pages 50 and 59, left)
Celeste Cooper
The Cooper Group
Boston, MA
(617) 426-3865

(page 53)
Judi Cunningham
Chez Joli
Winnetka, IL
(708) 446-2522

(page 56)
Blair Ballard and Associates
Laguna Beach, CA
(714) 494-8093

(page 58)
Siegel & Strain
Emeryville, CA
(510) 547-8092

(page 60, right)
Interior Consultants
Salem, NY
(914) 533-2275

(page 61)
Van Martin-Rowe
Pasadena, CA
(818) 577-4736

(page 63)
Powell/Kleinschmidt
Chicago, IL
(312) 642-6450

(page 64, right)
Richar Interiors
Chicago, IL
(312) 951-0924

(page 66)
Charles Damga, designer
Damga Design
New York, NY
(212) 570-1439

(page 68)
Ginsburg Development
   Corporation
Hawthorne, NY
(914) 747-3600

PHOTOGRAPHY CREDITS

© William Abranowicz: p. 9,
   46 left

© Philip Beaurline: p. 16 right,
   24

Crandall and Crandall
   Associates:
   © Knopf: p. 18;
   © Pallette: p. 22 left;
   © Oldham: p. 30;
   © Neimann: p. 56

© Daniel Eifert: Design: Joseph
   L. Roman: p. 40, 49

© Phillip Ennis: p. 26, 59;
   Design: Mojo Stumer
   Associates: p. 20; Design:
   Audio/Video Interiors:
   p. 25; Design: KJS
   Interiors: p. 31 right;
   Design: Mariette Himes,
   ASID, Gomez Associates:
   p. 37; Design: Gail Green
   Interior Design: p. 48

Esto Photographics:
   © Peter Aaron: p. 63;
   © Otto Baitz: p. 19 left,
      44 left, 65;
   © Mark Darley: p. 15
      right, 17, 42, 58;
   © Jeff Goldberg: p. 8,
      16 left ;
   © Scott Frances: p. 13,
      43 right

© Tria Giovan: p. 22 right, 38,
   41 right, 55

© Jennifer Levy: p. 19 right;
   Design: Keith Hone: p. 14;
   Design: Maxine Ordesky:
   p. 29 left

© Richard Mandelkorn: Stedila
   Design, Inc: p. 43; Design:
   Celeste Cooper: p. 50

Courtesy of Herman Miller,
   Inc./Photography by Nick
   Merrick/Hedrick Blessing:
   p. 6, 28, 34, 62

© Superstock: p. 41 left, 64 left

© Peter Paige: Damga Design:
   p. 66

© Robert Perron: Design: J.P.
   Franzen Associates: p. 31
   left

© David Phelps, courtesy
   Woman's Day magazine:
   Design: Charles Riley: p.
   29 right; Design: Van
   Martin-Rowe: p. 61

Courtesy of Richar Interiors/
   Photography by James
   Yochum: p. 64 right

© Eric Roth: p. 32, 45; Design:
   Anne Lenox, Partners in
   Design: p. 10; Design:
   Peter Wheeler: p. 23

© Bill Rothschild: Design:
   Charlotte Moss &
   Company: p. 35; Design:
   Vince Latucca: p. 47;
   Design: Interior
   Consultants: p. 60 right;
   Design: Ginsburg
   Development Corporation:
   p. 68

© Tim Street-Porter: Design:
   Nick Berman: p. 21, 57;
   Design: Frank Israel: p. 27;
   Design: Bobi Leonard
   Interiors: p. 2, 52; Design:
   Tracy Loeb/Forma
   Architects: p. 67; Design:
   Brindel Roberts: p. 51;
   Design: Sally Sirkin Lewis:
   p. 36, 69

© Jessie Walker Associates:
   p. 12, 54; Design: Judi
   Cunningham: p. 53

INDEX